MOVING
in the
PROPHETIC
ORDER IN THE CHURCH

MICHAEL BACON

Copyright © 2023 Michael Bacon.

All rights reserved. No part of this book may be reproduced, stored, or transmitted by any means—whether auditory, graphic, mechanical, or electronic—without written permission of both publisher and author, except in the case of brief excerpts used in critical articles and reviews. Unauthorized reproduction of any part of this work is illegal and is punishable by law.

Contents

Introduction v

Chapter 1   What is Prophecy? 1
Chapter 2   Types of Prophecy in the Church 5
Chapter 3   Is Prophecy for Today? 9
Chapter 4   Are Prophets for Today? 14
Chapter 5   Doctrines Matter 17
Chapter 6   Do not Despise Prophecy 20
Chapter 7   Why Prophecy is Often Despised 23
Chapter 8   Freedom Without the Chaos 33
Chapter 9   Build a Church that Allows the Holy Spirit to Move 38
Chapter 10 Put Structure and Protocols in Place 40
Chapter 11 Train, Equip, and Release 45
Chapter 12 Encourage the Body to Operate in Prophecy 49
Chapter 13 Have the Church and Prophets Judge the Words 52
Chapter 14 How to Correct and When to Correct 56
Chapter 15 Know who Labors Among You 59
Chapter 16 The Jezebel Spirit 63
Chapter 17 The Ahab Spirit 66
Chapter 18 The Absalom Spirit 70
Chapter 19 The Spirit of Witchcraft 73
Chapter 20 The Leviathan Spirit 78
Chapter 21 Be Watchful, Not Fearful 83
Chapter 22 Why Prophets and Pastors Often Clash 85
Chapter 23 It's Time to Bring Order Back to the Church 88

Introduction

I remember when I was first introduced to the gifts of the Spirit, particularly the prophetic, back in 1990. I was a recently converted Baptist, who had been taught that prophecy was not applicable anymore. In fact, I was taught that all the prophets and apostles had passed away, based on 1 Corinthians 13, and that these gifts were no longer relevant today. When I received my first word from God through another person, one might have expected me to approach it with skepticism and a critical mindset, given my denominational beliefs. However, when I received the word, something within me leaped, and I could feel God's presence as the person delivered the message to my life.

Honestly, I found myself torn between skepticism and a lingering curiosity. A significant part of me questioned whether there was more to God than what I had been taught. Specifically, I wondered if God continued to communicate with His people in the present day, or if the Bible was the ultimate and final revelation from God for our lives. Despite being a new convert and actively involved in serving God through a homeless ministry and church activities, I experienced moments of emptiness. I often wondered whether God was aware of my struggles and cared about the challenges I faced in my life. There were many times when I desperately needed guidance and encouragement, especially when it became difficult to discern God's voice for myself.

However, within the Baptist denomination, the prevailing belief was that God communicates solely through the Bible.

Consequently, I found myself wrestling with a great deal of confusion. The Bible described various spiritual gifts that the apostles utilized and indicated that we too would have the opportunity to operate in them. However, many within the church were asserting that these gifts were no longer relevant. The same held true for gifts like speaking in tongues and healing. This uncertainty even led me to question the validity of Mark 16:17-18 in the context of our lives. If prophets and apostles were no longer present, and if prophecy and healing were no longer considered applicable, then why did the Bible contain so much content related to these topics?

> *Mark 16:17-18*
> *[17] And these signs shall follow them that believe; In my name shall they cast out devils; they shall speak with new tongues;*
> *[18] They shall take up serpents; and if they drink any deadly thing, it shall not hurt them; they shall lay hands on the sick, and they shall recover.*

Looking back on that time, I can now clearly see how God was actively working and orchestrating events in my life. Please don't misunderstand me; I firmly believe that every spiritual gift must align with the teachings of the Bible. I consider the Bible to be the most essential tool at our disposal. However, I always had this sense that there was more to it, and more to God. At that time, and even now I was of the belief that God is still communicating with people in the present day. Additionally, I had a strong desire for a deeper connection with God and a greater understanding of the blessings He had in store for me.

When I initially received a personal prophecy, it not only proved to be remarkably accurate but also seemed to infuse new life into me. It brought forth a renewed sense of hope and encouragement, motivating me to persevere along the path God had laid out for me. Little did I realize at the time that God would eventually use me in the realm of prophetic gifts. In truth, I had very little awareness of this possibility back then.

Shortly after receiving my initial prophecy. I participated in a joint military exercise that involved the Air Force, Navy, and Army, while I was serving in the Air Force. During that time, I was temporarily stationed at Little Creek Naval Base in Virginia, where I was assigned to a dormitory-style room with five other people, featuring three bunk beds.

Interestingly, this turned out to be a significant and divine appointment in my life. Among my roommates, there was a gentleman from a Pentecostal Holiness church who happened to be my roommate. I do not believe this was a coincidence, but part of God's plan for my life. He swiftly discerned my Baptist background and began attempting to discuss certain revelations that the Lord had shown him concerning me. However, he made it clear that he wouldn't disclose the details of what the Lord had revealed. Instead, he challenged me to spend a night in prayer and seek God for His plans in my life. Frankly, this man kind of rubbed me the wrong way. I mean who did he think he was. God doesn't talk to people that way today, does He? Again, leaning on what I had been taught in my denomination.

Yet, to shut his mouth, I stayed up that night to seek the Lord. Now, I didn't try too hard mind you. I was a bible popper back in the day. I would pop my bible open and say okay God speak to me. Oddly, strangely, God did talk to me that night through bible popping. I am telling you that every time I opened that bible up in a random place, there were be two words that would leap off the pages.

Those two words were contrary to what my denomination believed in. I kept seeing over and over the words, "prophet", and "apostle". The following day, my roommate turned to me and inquired, "What did God reveal about your future last night?" His question was rather vexing to me. I simply gazed at him and responded, "It wasn't God. They are all deceased now." I conveyed my disbelief that it had been a divine message. In response, he burst into laughter, intensifying my irritation. He persistently affirmed, "You did hear from God." Overwhelmed with frustration, I chose to disengage completely from the conversation. I maintained the belief that this individual lacked a genuine connection to God's voice, and I remained skeptical of the events involving my Bible from the previous night.

As it turns out, the joke was on me, because today, I am now ordained as an apostle and prophet. I can now comprehend what God had revealed to him back then, even though I was unable to perceive or receive it at the time. My faith in those moments was inadequate, but God used that man as an instrument. This story remains etched in my memory, and while I may have mocked him back then, I would eagerly embrace him and express my gratitude if given the chance today, perhaps even in heaven one day.

The undeniable truth is that prophecy can wield immense power within the church, offering profound encouragement and the potential to transform lives. The Bible explicitly advises us not to disregard prophecy, and we should heed this guidance. However, it is also true that there are numerous instances of misuse and abuse of prophecy within the contemporary church.

Let's begin by establishing that one does not require ordination as a prophet to engage in prophecy. In fact, God can choose and use anyone as a vessel for prophetic messages, and He has done so on numerous occasions. Furthermore, it's imperative to emphasize that our reverence and worship should be directed solely towards God, rather than the person delivering a prophecy or the gift of prophecy itself. Those who prophesy merely serve as conduits through which God conveys His will and purpose to individuals.

In this book, I will establish a foundation for understanding how to engage with the gift of prophecy, explaining its role within the modern church, and how to create the right atmosphere for its operation. My hope is that pastors and leaders will be open to allowing God's movement through the gifts of the spirit, while maintaining discernment in distinguishing what is genuinely from God and what is not.

Providing instruction to the church about the appropriate and inappropriate methods of participating in prophecy is vital. This includes guidance on when to exercise restraint and when to correct, along with the establishment of protocols that protect both the individual engaged in prophecy and the local church. This is particularly important because prophets have the potential to disrupt the harmony of a church by delivering inaccurate prophecies, having impure motives, nurturing critical attitudes, or introducing negative spiritual influences. Instead of suppressing the gift, our primary objective should be to cultivate a safe environment that allows the presence of God to thrive among us.

chapter

What is Prophecy?

Let's begin with an exploration of what prophecy signifies and its relevance to today's church. To put it simply, prophecy entails God communicating with an individual and conveying His divine will and purpose through that individual to His church. However, it encompasses much more than mere words. When God speaks, His utterances not only declare what He intends to accomplish, but also releases the substance of His will into the earthly realm. The moment He speaks His words, everything He envisions and declares becomes an active force in our lives. His words possess tremendous power, just as He has taught us that our tongues hold the power of life and death. As we are made in His image, our words also bear influence. However, the most important point to be made here is that when God speaks, His words instantly enter our reality. However, the timing and method by which His words come to fruition often vary according to His divine will. It is important to understand that nothing happens outside of His will and purpose. Even adverse events are subject to God and His sovereign will, which holds ultimate authority and jurisdiction over all earthly powers, including Satan and his demonic realm.

If we go back to the book of Genesis, we can see how God worked: He made everything on Earth by simply saying it. He spoke, and things like Adam and Eve, the Earth, stars, animals, and everything else came to be. When God said something, it happened. This has been the divine pattern since the dawn of time. Unfortunately, humanity often underestimates the potency of God's words and their profound significance not only for our existence but also for our future. His voice holds unrivaled dominion, and when He speaks, all of creation, from the Earth and the cosmos to humanity, angels, and even demons, must heed His command.

Today, we observe that adversaries, including governments, are inten-sifying their efforts to stifle the voice of God. Even some churches are turning away from prophecy and the direct voice of God in favor of human doctrines and opinions, distancing themselves from the "Thus saith the Lord" principle. The Bible explicitly instructs us not to despise prophecy, and it also encourages us to desire prophesy. 1 Corinthians 14:1 "Follow after charity, and desire spiritual gifts, but rather that ye may prophesy."

Yet, there exists a pervasive fear of prophecy today, leading many churches to avoid it altogether. Others doubt its relevance in the present day. Among the churches that do permit prophecy, numerous instances of its misuse and abuse can be observed. Some Christians even elevate the gift itself, instead of understanding that God can employ any means to communicate His message. It is God Himself who deserves our worship, as He is the bestower of the gift.

The Bible also teaches that through authentic prophecy, individuals are edified, encouraged, and sometimes corrected by God. Throughout history we see that every divine move is preceded by a prophetic declaration. When God speaks, both the Earth and the heavens respond. Consequently, we must allow God to speak and to manifest His will within the church and among His people. I have personally witnessed God speaking through various means, including teaching, preaching, evangelism, and worship. Some may even categorize these as "prophetic teaching, prophetic preaching, prophetic evangelism, prophetic healing, prophetic deliverance, and prophetic worship." It's essentially God expressing Himself through His divine actions. For instance, in the context of healing, God often imparts words of knowledge about someone's physical ailment, and after the proclamation of this revelation, healing ensues. This exemplifies God conveying a message to someone and subsequently bringing it to fruition in the natural realm. In prophetic evangelism, God provides insights into an individual's life, leading to salvation, deliverance, and healing. In prophetic teaching, God imparts words and revelations while someone teaches, rather than the individual planning their message in advance.

Prophecy carries as much divine authority as the Bible itself. However, prophecy should never contradict, supplant, or undermine the written Word of God; it should always complement or fulfill it. I've heard some ministers assert that the Bible is the only true Word of God, a statement we must scrutinize as it is not a correct doctrine. The Bible represents the Word of God transmitted through God-inspired individuals who were moved by the Holy Spirit to record the books of the Bible. This process is not vastly different from the release of prophetic words today. For example, John entered into a visionary experience and recorded what he witnessed, similarly to Ezekiel. Thus, stating that the Bible is the sole true Word of God is an erroneous teaching as clearly God used men to write the bible, and prophecy continues to be a means of communication from God to the church.

Nevertheless, we must discern the source of every prophecy, whether it originates from the Holy Spirit, the human mind, the flesh, or the demonic realm. Each prophecy should undergo examination and testing to ensure that we exclusively receive what God has communicated to His church. Satan excels in counterfeiting spiritual gifts, making it imperative that we employ our gifts of discernment and wisdom to discern the true and acceptable Word of God.

Another area of importance is to recognize that one does not become a prophet merely by prophesying. Some individuals are called to the office of a prophet, while others may have the gift of prophecy without occupying the office of a prophet. Both the prophet and the person with the gift of prophecy can prophesy as the Holy Spirit prompts them. God shows no favoritism and can use anyone, even employing a donkey to convey His message. The individual who prophesies should always attribute the gift to God and never attempt to misrepresent Him or steal His glory.

Lastly, I firmly believe that the forthcoming move of God will be initiated through the words of His prophets. God is presently communicating about what lies ahead. The church must exercise caution not to seek out false prophets who disseminate messages that cater to human desires. Instead, we must remain receptive to whatever God desires to convey in this moment, including messages of rebuke and correction. The next move of God may likely involve purifying the church to prepare it for what lies ahead. Thankfully, I believe God is speaking more today than ever before. In the subsequent sections of this book, we will delve deeper into the protocols governing prophecy.

chapter 2

Types of Prophecy in the Church

There are a variety of prophets, diverse prophetic anointings, and types of prophecies. Occasionally, we become accustomed to a particular type or two of prophecies, yet God has a greater purpose for the prophetic in our times. Regrettably, the church has restricted God in terms of where it permits Him to communicate. In reality, God is constantly speaking and making His gifts available, but often, we turn away from what He is offering us. It's imperative that we remain open to whatever God has in store for us, while simultaneously guarding against falsehood. This can be challenging, but it should not serve as a reason to stifle the prophetic within the church. In fact, God cautions us against disregarding prophecy.

> *1 Thessalonians 5:20-21*
> *[20] Despise not prophesyings. [21] Prove all things; hold fast that which is good.*

As mentioned, there are several ways that God is speaking to the church, and several types of prophecies in operation that include: corporate words, personal prophecy, foretelling words (speaking of the future), forthtelling words (speaking into the present), as well as words of encouragement and edification, and even correction and reproof. Each type of prophecy has a particular purpose and may even have a different flow to it. There are also personal prophecies and corporate words.

Corporate words are important because they are given openly for all to judge and discern. They are not meant to give in private. They require that all hear and discern by the Holy Spirit if they are of the Lord or not. In most cases, even personal prophecies should be given openly for all to judge so there is no confusion and the sheep can be protected. Some words are speaking about the past, some about the present situations, and in other cases about the future.

Occasionally, God may even have a corrective word for the body or a person. These words may or may not be given publicly depending on what the Holy Spirit is saying. Most of the times these types of words are shared with leadership before being shared with the body or the person. This is to bring protection as to the accuracy of the word and the spirit in which it is being given.

Forthtelling involves receiving a message about someone's life, either pertaining to the present or the past. It becomes evident that only God could possess knowledge of the information conveyed, and the person delivering the message has no prior awareness of the individual's life before sharing the word. Often, these messages relate to the person's current circumstances. On the other hand, foretelling pertains to speaking about future events. These prophecies are more challenging to evaluate since their authenticity can only be confirmed when they unfold. In contemporary times, many individuals prophesy about future occurrences, yet a significant portion of these prophecies may turn out to be false, with no certainty of their accuracy unless they come to fruition.

I frequently hear of prophecies concerning matters such as cars, houses, spouses, children, jobs, and more. However, it's important to note that making such grand promises without the guidance of the Holy Spirit can have severe consequences. People can make all sorts of claims, but unless it genuinely originates from God, those promises will remain unfulfilled and possibly derail people's lives. Prophecy can also be dangerous especially if it is a directional word. A word that brings direction can cause a person to chase after that prophecy to make it happen. This could alter the course of their lives. The church should be warned not to chase prophecies, but to chase after God. We are not to make words happen. We are to judge the word, pray over the word, and allow God to make it happen. In rare cases, God may or may not have us step out in an act of faith to do something in response to that prophecy.

I have seen people get words about marriage and expect God to send the person the next day. In some cases, the person waited years before they came. In other cases, I have seen someone get a word about getting married and the next week latch on to someone saying this is the person God sent when they are actually a counterfeit. We must be careful to pray over every word we get and to trust God to bring it to pass. As to the counterfeit words, or the words we are unsure about, we should put them on a shelf and not receive them unless God tells us they are from Him.

Words of encouragement are just that. They encourage the person. They cause the person to want to obey God and serve Him. They may also encourage them to continue on in the faith and not to quit. These words are so essential to the local body. The enemy is chasing down and discouraging many in the body of Christ. Words of encouragement should not be undervalued. They are so important. To hear that God is still with us and that He knows what we are going through can encourage us to continue to run the race and to fight the good fight of faith. It is in the times of uncertainty or darkness that many fall away or quit just short of the finish line.

One of the most powerful types of prophecies to me is when God speaks to His intercessors. He speaks things to His intercessors so that they will pray and war for what He is saying to His church. These are in the form of words of knowledge or visions a lot of times. There are intercessors and there are prophetic intercessors. Prophetic intercessors do major damage to the works of darkness on the earth. God speaks, then the intercessors speak what He said and pray it into existence. There are several factors here. First, God said it. Second, the intercessor agreed with it. Third, the intercessor births the word by speaking it into the atmosphere. Forth, the intercessor then prays the word into existence, even birthing it forth.

We as the church do not fully understand that God has sent different types of prophecy to shift the atmosphere and to release His will on the earth. Too many leaders are rejecting the prophetic and therefore are resisting the Holy Spirit and shutting down the works that He desires to do on the earth. The earth was formed because God spoke. Every miracle we read about was spoken forth by God. When we reject His words we reject His will and purpose and through our unbelief stop a move of God. Churches all over the world are praying for revival, but how many of them allow God to speak any more? Most churches have shut down the gift of prophecy altogether. We just need to allow God to move, and obey Him when He speaks. Then the church as we know it will be forever changed.

3
chapter

Is Prophecy for Today?

Does today's church bear any resemblance to the early church described in the book of Acts? Today's church seems to have lost its way, having grown feeble, ineffectual, and apprehensive of engaging with the world. It appears to have transformed into an institution or business entity that shies away from its duty to demonstrate God's love through acts of healing, deliverance, and the manifestation of signs, wonders, and miracles. In numerous churches across America, the gifts of the Spirit are even prohibited. The acceptance of prophecy is often a divisive matter among churches, with some denominations embracing it and others outrightly rejecting it. Depending on the denomination, the practice and tolerance of these gifts can vary greatly. Now, let's explore some doctrinal reasons that have led to the rejection of contemporary prophecy, citing 1 Corinthians 13:8-10 as an example.

> *1 Corinthians 13:8-10*
> *⁸ Charity never faileth: but whether there be prophecies, they shall fail; whether there be tongues, they shall cease; whether there be knowledge, it shall vanish away. ⁹ For we know in part, and we prophesy in part. ¹⁰ But when that which is perfect is come, then that which is in part shall be done away.*

In verse 10 of 1 Corinthians 13, it states, "but when that which is perfect is come, then that which is in part shall be done away." When you consider this, what do you believe it means? Most denominations concur that the term "perfect" refers to Jesus. Therefore, when Jesus arrives, the partial will be replaced. In verse 9, it explicitly mentions that we have limited knowledge and prophesy partially. This is because God communicates with each of us, providing a portion of His message so that together we can grasp the complete picture of His intentions.

The disagreement among denominations isn't about Jesus being perfect; there's consensus on that aspect. The real debate centers on the timing of when these spiritual gifts will cease on Earth. Some denominations interpret 1 Corinthians 13:10 as signifying that when Jesus came to Earth the first time, He fulfilled this verse, implying that now, since He has ascended to heaven, the gifts are no longer necessary. In contrast, another group of denominations interprets this verse to mean that we will continue to operate in these gifts until Jesus returns for the second time. This might appear to be a minor dispute, but the answer to this question or interpretation can significantly influence the direction of the church, for better or worse. So, what is the correct answer, and why does it truly matter? Let's delve deeper into this matter.

Which denominations are witnessing the power of God through the manifestation of signs, wonders, miracles, and healings? Additionally, which denominations diligently preach the Word of God, yet little seems to be happening in terms of power? Despite their growing numbers, why do so many individuals within these denominations suffer from illness, fatigue, and despair? Has God's communication been restricted to only the pastor? What about the other four spiritual offices? Have they become obsolete as well?

I want to make it clear that I am not attacking denominations, but many of them have gradually pushed the Holy Spirit out of the church, creating a structure that prohibits or hinders His work. It also seems that many denominations are fearful of allowing others to be used by God, often because they have witnessed instances of gift misuse or encountered false gifts, which has instilled fear of error. Others adhere to what they were taught in seminary, believing that spiritual gifts are no longer relevant, and as a result, they reject them.

Most church services follow a similar pattern every week, often consisting of three or four songs, followed by an offering, and then a sermon from the pastor. Yet, all the diverse gifts within the body of Christ remain largely untapped. This is noticeable in many churches, where people do not feel free or empowered to operate in their gifts. Many have prophetic words that could bring healing, restoration, and encouragement to the church, but these words remain unshared because there is no place for them to be expressed. While some denominations allow these gifts in small group settings, the majority are uncomfortable even with that level of openness.

Due to these circumstances, individuals often find that the very thing they need from God is withheld from them. The pastor, while important, is just one piece of the puzzle. We require the other four spiritual offices and all the gifts in operation to gain a comprehensive understanding and to fully experience the presence of God that we need. Unfortunately, some churches centralize everything around the pastor and the pastor's teachings, often sidelining intercessors and prophetic voices out of fear of losing control over the church. Sadly, they fail to recognize that God imparts His message to us individually, using each person as a part to accomplish His complete work.

Regrettably, denominations that believe prophecy is no longer relevant or necessary for God's work are following incorrect doctrine. This erroneous doctrine leads to spiritual and physical suffering when God could have offered healing and deliverance. My question to each reader is: What is the truth? Should we reject prophecy today? Is it a genuine gift from God, or has it become obsolete? Is prophecy still essential? Does God continue to speak to His people through prophecy?

In the very next chapter of 1 Corinthians 14, Paul clearly states that we are to desire to prophesy. He even talks about the gifts of tongues, which many churches have rejected altogether.

> *1 Corinthians 14:1-5*
> *[1] Follow after charity, and desire spiritual gifts, but rather that ye may prophesy. [2] For he that speaketh in an unknown tongue speaketh not unto men, but unto God: for no man understandeth him; howbeit in the spirit he speaketh mysteries. [3] But he that prophesieth speaketh unto men to edification, and exhortation, and comfort. [4] He that speaketh in an unknown tongue edifieth himself; but he that prophesieth edifieth the church. [5] I would that ye all spake with tongues but rather that ye prophesied: for greater is he that prophesieth than he that speaketh with tongues, except he interpret, that the church may receive edifying.*

Paul not only says to prophesy, but to desire the gift of prophecy. He later goes on to explain why prophecy is needed in the church. Prophecy provides the church with *edification, and exhortation, and comfort.* If this is true, then why aren't we allowing this gift in the church? When people speak in tongues – through their prayer language it edifies themselves. When people prophesy the church body is edified.

There are two uses of tongues by the way. One is our prayer language where Holy Spirit prays through our tongue for us and His will to be done in our lives. That is edifying ourselves. No one else in the room is edified by those tongues. However, when God moves on us to speak in a tongue a prophetic word, it would require an interpretation so that it would be edifying to the church body.

> *1 Corinthians 14:4*
> *[4] He that speaketh in an unknown tongue edifieth himself; but he that prophesieth edifieth the church.*

Certainly, the gifts of the Spirit and prophecy hold great significance within today's church. Their importance is underscored by Paul's extensive teaching on the matter in 1 Corinthians 14. If these gifts were not to be part of the church, they wouldn't have been mentioned in chapter 14 and throughout the rest of the New Testament. From my personal perspective, I fail to see how the church can effectively navigate the challenges of the last days without the full operation of the gifts of the Holy Spirit. How can the church stand against the spirit of the anti-Christ without the complete power and presence of the Holy Spirit? I firmly believe that the gifts are more essential than ever and will continue to operate fully until the moment of the rapture. It is only when God has withdrawn His people and His Spirit from the earth that the anti-Christ will have unrestricted control until Christ returns with His mighty and victorious army.

4
chapter

Are Prophets for Today?

In many denominations, the term "prophet" is openly discredited. At the same time, there is a growing trend of individuals adopting titles like apostle and prophet without a genuine calling from God. Some even exploit these titles to manipulate and gather large offerings through prophecy. Many believe that having such titles will grant them credibility in the Christian community. Regrettably, the title of "servant" is seldom embraced, though it is a role that every believer is called to, regardless of their specific calling or title.

However, the more significant issue, as mentioned earlier, is the need for a diversity of offices within the church, beyond just the role of pastor. Many denominations adopt a single-fold approach, with the church revolving primarily around the pastor's role. In such models, there is often little to no accountability for the pastor, no apostles to bring order, no prophets to provide edification or exhortation, and frequently, no teachers to impart sound doctrine. While evangelists may operate outside the church, God's original design did not intend for the pastor to be the sole leader in the church. Unfortunately, some people tend to idolize the pastor, making everything revolve around their teachings and beliefs.

Control issues have infiltrated many churches, often stemming from ignorance. Sometimes, control may be rooted in the pastor's legitimate concern for protecting the congregation. However, just as parents must eventually allow their children to learn from others and from God, pastors should also permit others to speak into the lives of their congregants. Overprotectiveness can hinder spiritual growth and limit one's ability to serve God fully. Ultimately, God is the ultimate parent and teacher, and we should allow others to contribute to our spiritual growth.

Likewise, in the Kingdom of God, pastors can only take the congregation so far. Their role primarily involves safeguarding, nurturing, and caring for the flock. Interestingly, the Bible doesn't depict pastors as performing signs, wonders, and miracles; these manifestations are often associated more with apostles and prophets. Each office carries distinct mantles, anointings, and giftings. Apostles can release anointings in the church that pastors cannot, and prophets can deliver words of edification, exhortation, and correction that pastors may not provide. It is crucial to recognize that these offices play integral roles in the foundation and fulfillment of God's commission for the church.

Due to past abuses of the prophetic, many denominations today do not acknowledge prophets as part of God's plan. This fear-based approach often stems from leadership's desire to maintain control. Yet, the church is suffering in various areas due to its rejection of this gift and office, as mentioned earlier. Churches worldwide fervently pray for revival but simultaneously reject the instruments God has provided to ignite that revival.

The challenge with this approach lies in the inconsistency. For instance, when pastors make errors or lose their way, we don't conclude that pastors are no longer needed in the church. While there have been false prophets and instances of false prophecy that have caused harm, it is not a valid reason to expel all prophecy and prophets from our congregations. This irony is evident. Regardless of the office, people are fallible. We cannot allow fear of the false to lead us to reject the true gifts and offices altogether. We cannot amputate a part of our body and expect to function fully as a body. Instead, we should aim for greater discernment and protective measures while permitting God to continue using prophecy and prophets as He deems fit.

The office of the prophet remains relevant today. God speaks through His prophets, whether we acknowledge it or not. We cannot reject a portion of God's gifts and expect revival. Let us strive for orderliness, relying on wisdom and discernment rather than living in fear. The Lord has revealed that the enemy seeks to eliminate intercessors and prophets from the church. Without intercessors in prayer and prophets with discernment, the church would be powerless against the enemy. Moreover, without apostolic authority, there is no governance to oppose the enemy effectively. I firmly believe that genuine prophets are emerging, driven not by titles, fame, position, or money, but solely by the desire to fulfill the Father's will. Past abuses and fear should not prevent us from embracing all that God has in store for our lives and the church.

5
chapter

Doctrines Matter

As a young man, I experienced my salvation in my early twenties within the Baptist denomination. My time as a Baptist taught me valuable lessons. Among the various denominations, I consider Baptists to be particularly evangelistic. They emphasize the study of the Bible and the proclamation of God's word. I was trained to engage in door-to-door evangelism and became adept at addressing any objections raised by unbelievers during our conversations. My approach often centered on conveying the urgency of turning to God to avoid the consequences of not accepting Christ, with a message largely grounded in fear.

This early period of my ministry began in the streets of San Antonio, where I focused on reaching people for Christ. However, there were two significant aspects missing from my spiritual journey: a deeper relationship with God and the empowerment of the Holy Spirit. At that time, my ministry was based on what I had been taught, and I lacked the ability to hear from God and exercise authority over demonic forces. It was only after receiving the infilling of the Holy Spirit that I began to witness victories over the forces of darkness.

I recall a specific incident when I brought a group of homeless men to a church. During their visit, one of the men experienced a demonic episode in the church parking lot. A deacon who witnessed the episode reacted with fear and scolded me, suggesting that I had endangered the entire church by bringing this man to church. This encounter marked a turning point for me, as I realized that my beliefs and approach were different from those of the Baptist church I attended. I confronted the deacon, asking him, "What are you afraid of? It's just a demon, and don't we have power over demons?" His response was to walk away. Following this incident, I approached the pastor and shared that the Lord was leading me to leave the church. God had directed me to a prophetic church, but the pastor rebuked me, accusing me of seeking signs, wonders, and miracles. Looking back, I believe he may have had a point. I yearned to witness God's power in action because that is the calling for all believers.

The teachings and beliefs we hold are of great significance. If we adhere to incorrect beliefs, we can hinder God's will in our lives. Some churches and denominations have embraced erroneous teachings and human doctrines, limiting their ability to fulfill God's plans. We are all susceptible to falling into this trap in various ways. Often, we realize that we have adopted certain beliefs based on prior teachings or books we've read, instead of seeking God directly on the matter. We should diligently seek God and His will in every aspect of our lives, even in areas where we believe we are firmly in the right. It is possible to discover that we have been walking in error or that God has more to reveal beyond the confines of our existing understanding.

We should not rely solely on the teachings of men. Instead, we should engage in the study of God's Word, striving to be approved by

Him. Moreover, we must allow the Holy Spirit to teach us and illuminate the Scriptures. Through His guidance, we can unlock mysteries and insights we have never encountered before. I firmly believe that the revelation and transformative power of God's Word can impact lives and redirect the course of our destinies.

6
chapter

Do not Despise Prophecy

What does it mean to despise prophecy and why do so many reject the gift altogether? Paul clearly teaches that we are to pursue the love of God, and His gifts, but even more so that we desire to prophesy.

> *1 Corinthians 14:1*
> *¹ Follow after charity, and desire spiritual gifts, but rather that ye may prophesy.*

Why would Paul emphasize this point to the church if the gift of prophecy was no longer relevant today? I am of the opinion, that Paul foresaw that many might reject this gift. His message to the church was clear: we should earnestly wish for God to communicate through His people. However, it is disheartening to witness numerous churches and leaders rejecting this gift outright, even prohibiting its practice within the local church. There are various reasons for this, which I will elaborate on shortly. Nevertheless, it is crucial to remember that the Bible also instructs us not to hold prophecy in contempt.

> *1 Thessalonians 5:20-21*
> *[20] Despise not prophesyings. [21] Prove all things; hold fast that which is good.*

Paul's teaching emphasizes that we should not hold contempt for or reject the gift of prophecy; instead, we should test and examine these gifts. The primary goal of this book is to educate the church on how to evaluate these gifts properly. It's essential to understand what God's teachings are and how the gifts of the Spirit should be employed within the local church. We cannot allow the fear of prophecy to hinder the church's progress into what God has in store for this generation. While there are valid concerns that some pastors have regarding prophecy, these concerns should never outweigh God's word and/or His will.

We must confront any areas where we harbor negative feelings toward God's gifts and restore order and correction within the church. The first step is to return to the teachings of God's word, repent for our fears and disobedience, and allow the Holy Spirit to move freely within the church.

Several things have led churches and pastors to reject prophecy, and some of these concerns are valid. However, these concerns should not be excuses to hinder the operation of God's gifts. Many churches pray for a divine outpouring, yet they stifle the Holy Spirit's work through the gifts of the Spirit, ultimately delaying God's will.

When we despise prophecy, we are essentially rejecting a vital part of what God has bestowed upon the church. This rejection deprives the church of an essential gift that serves to edify and uplift God's people. Moreover, prophecy plays a crucial role in releasing God's plans to the church, as specific moves of God are often spoken before they come to pass. God has always communicated His intentions before acting, starting from the Garden of Eden and continuing to this day.

Disregarding prophecy is equivalent to hating a portion of God's gifts. Imagine if I despised one of my limbs, like my arm or leg. Would it be wise for me to amputate it? What consequences would I face if I were to remove a limb? Could my body function effectively, or would I struggle to perform essential tasks? Likewise, we cannot afford to go without the word of the Lord. God continues to speak through His prophets today, and prophecy remains relevant and indispensable in the kingdom of God.

chapter 7

Why Prophecy is Often Despised

Afundamental question we should ponder is: why? Why does prophecy face such widespread disdain from numerous individuals, churches, and denominations? Let's delve into some of the factors contributing to this prevailing sentiment in our contemporary context.

- **Previous abuses/errors In prophecy**

    One of the most common issues concerning prophecy is the abuse of it. Somewhere in the church history a person moving in the prophetic has either abused the gift, or caused some type of issue in the church, and now leadership has shut down all prophecy as a safety precaution. By removing prophecy altogether, they think they are reducing any potential conflicts surrounding prophecy. The problem is that this is a controlling spirit that is choosing to ignore God's word and reject His other gifts. By doing so the church moves from being multi-dimensional to one-dimensional and often suffers due to the lack of spiritual gifts in operation. Typically, the pastor role then takes on areas of responsibility for spiritually feeding people that God never called them to.

- **Leadership is afraid of losing control**

    The leadership of the church is afraid of losing control over the congregation or afraid of the sheep being hurt. In either case it is a fear-based scenario that produces dependency on the pastor and limits the gifts of God in the body of Christ. Controlling spirits often quench the Holy Spirit and hinder a move of God in a church or region. We can allow the gifts of God to move without fear when we have a good foundation in our churches and ministries where we teach people what is in order and what is out of order. We can also bring correction in love when abuses are seen. One of the things that is interesting is that prophets and prophecy has been pushed out of the church due to the fear of missing it or abuses of the office or gift, yet pastors still exist and are welcomed even though many pastors have made mistakes or sinned themselves. We don't throw out all the pastors due to the mistakes of other pastors, do we?

- **Spirit of competition**

    Instead of the offices and gifts flowing together, people are operating with wrong motives and trying to have people follow them instead of Holy Spirit. Think about how often we have seen people in the local body competing for positions and titles. Now think about the conflict that exists between churches where one church is trying to compete with another church for people. I have even witnessed pastors approaching members from other churches trying to recruit them. The spirit of competition is very strong in churches. Now take that same spirit of competition and you can see where pastors and prophets begin to compete for the affections of the people. Pastors are trying to protect the people, prophets are trying to speak the word of God to the people, but if not careful many people will be attracted to the prophetic gift and follow the prophet instead of following God. There have even been church splits over this. So, I understand why there is concern, but often the pastor becomes jealous of the prophetic gift and wants the attention back on themselves. So, a war ensues and the people are dragged along for the ride so to speak. I have even heard it said that pastors and prophets do not get along. The problem with that is that every church needs both a pastor and a prophet. In many ways they balance each other out.

- **Fear of error**

    Earlier we mentioned a fear of losing control, but now I want to talk about the fear of error. Some churches and ministries are so scared to make a mistake that they miss the move of God. I understand the need to keep the sanctity and integrity of the word of God and to keep order in the church. I agree that we must have order and truth in every church and ministry. However, due to the fear of error or wrong prophecies, the leadership some churches limit prophecy or the use of it. They say they do this to protect the church potential error or abuses of the gift. That is like saying some food may not be good for you if you eat large amounts of it. The food itself is good, but the person has to be careful not to overeat. You don't cut the food out to protect a person from overeating now do you? Most people know they need some self-control and need to follow a diet which controls what they eat and how much. There are no food police that walk around and say don't eat that. Each person needs to be responsible for that. When it comes to prophecy we should not be stopping prophecy from happening in case someone misses it, but instead helping teach people how to discern and test the words they are hearing. If we as leaders teach people and equip them to operate in discernment then it would be hard for a false prophecy to go forth without a lot of alarms in the spirit going off. Fear is the opposite of faith. It is empowering Satan versus trusting God. Don't let the fear of error stop God from speaking to His people. Teach people what prophecy is, how to walk in it, how to discern and test the word, and what to do with it if it is error.

- **Wrong doctrine**

    This is one of the most prevalent reasons why prophecy does not exist in most of today's churches. Somewhere in history the denomination came to the conclusion that prophecy is not for today. Many denominations base this on 1 Corinthians 13 which talks about when the perfect comes that these things will pass away. Many believe wrongly that when Jesus came to earth that was the perfect that came and that the gifts are no longer needed in the body of Christ. That is why we don't see the level of signs, wonders and miracles that the early church saw in their time. This wrong doctrine has rendered the church powerless against the works of darkness. Until Christ returns for His bride we need all the gifts He has given us to do the work of God. He even told us that these signs will follow those that believe. I believe that "when the perfect comes" is referring to the return of Christ or the rapture. At that time the gifts will no longer be needed. Ironically, 1 Corinthians 14 and later talks about how we should all desire to prophesy. So, this doctrine is clearly wrong. We should all search the word out and make sure we have correct doctrines.

- **Jealousy of the gift/office**

  Regrettably, envy often takes root within the church community. There are instances where prophets harbor jealousy towards pastors, and conversely, pastors may feel envious of prophets. Nevertheless, the spirit of jealousy has no rightful place within the church. Regrettably, it is one of the underlying causes behind pastors' reluctance to permit the operation of prophecy within the church. Some may seek to maintain their status as the center of attention or the ultimate authority in the church. Yet, we must remember that this is God's church, and it comprises five distinct offices, each with its own purpose and a shared responsibility for mutual accountability. This structure helps safeguard against pride, doctrinal errors, and spiritual misconduct.

- **Failure to recognize the value of the gift**

  Some ministries fail to recognize the significance of the prophetic gift. When the pastor or leadership lacks an understanding of its importance, they may discourage or even prohibit its use. For instance, if a minister belongs to a denomination that does not embrace or practice the prophetic gift, it may result in its non-utilization. Additionally, some churches may restrict prophecy to specific settings, such as prohibiting it during the main service and only permitting corporate prophecies during that time or reserving personal prophecies for after the service or small group gatherings. When we underestimate the value of the gift of prophecy, we limit the richness of our church services. However, I believe that every gift is valuable and should be valued and employed as the Holy Spirit guides. Our worship is not directed towards prophecy or any specific gift, but rather we allow the Holy Spirit to work through whomever He chooses, even during our services.

- **Religious spirit**

    Numerous Christians unknowingly find themselves operating under the influence of a religious spirit. The Bible instructs us that some individuals exhibit an appearance of godliness but reject its inherent power. They possess knowledge of God's Word, diligently follow their religious practices, yet refrain from allowing the gifts of the Spirit to manifest, thereby constraining the potential ways in which God can work. Many of these gatherings turn into mere religious rituals and can even become driven by the flesh. When God's presence becomes palpable, lives are transformed, and His power is evident through acts of healing, deliverance, and yes, prophecy. Prophecy often encounters resistance from religious spirits, which vehemently oppose any instance of God speaking beyond their established norms. In truth, a significant number of churches hinder the movement of the Holy Spirit due to the prevalence of religious spirits and related mindsets.

- **Lack of discernment**

    A significant factor contributing to the suppression and inhibition of prophecy lies in the absence of discernment within the church. When we possess discernment, we are unafraid of witnessing God releasing people in their giftings. Discernment empowers us to recognize anything that contradicts the Word of God or the leading of His Holy Spirit. Unfortunately, there is often a dearth of discernment concerning spirits within the church. Consequently, many churches shy away from embracing the gifts, fearing potential mishaps or harm to individuals. While their intention to safeguard is commendable, it ultimately hampers the growth and vitality of the church. To draw a parallel, consider how parents frequently struggle with the fear of letting their children mature and become more independent. Instead of attempting to exert excessive control over their children, parents should impart essential guidance and teach them the ways of discernment. This includes instructing them on how to discern whether a spiritual gift is from God or influenced by the enemy. Equipping them with discernment not only enables them to walk in the fullness of God's gifts but also safeguards them from harm.

- **Wrong Structure – Only the Pastor is allowed to speak**

    It has become quite common for congregation members to fixate on the role of the pastor and their pronouncements. However, we ought to question: To whom is the pastor held accountable? Where in the Bible do we find the pastor as the focal point of the church? It is crucial to remember that Jesus serves as the true center of the church, being the chief cornerstone. Additionally, the church's foundation rests upon the teachings of the prophets and apostles. Regrettably, the predominant emphasis often revolves around the pastor in many congregations. In such settings, the broader body of Christ may be precluded from sharing from the pulpit, with this privilege exclusively reserved for the pastor. This exclusion stems from the belief that God's voice can only be channeled through the pastor, as they are perceived as the sole authority within the church.

Let me clarify that I hold pastors in high regard, appreciating their sacrificial service to Christ and His people. Pastors shoulder a significant portion of the church's responsibilities and play a crucial leadership role. Nonetheless, it's essential to recognize that the multifaceted aspects of God's character are manifested through various offices and spiritual gifts. We should always bear in mind that the Bible instructs us on the diverse ways in which the Holy Spirit moves through individuals at different times. This movement follows a divine order, and it is our responsibility to align ourselves with God's established order. Consequently, we are called not only to honor one another, each respective office, and every spiritual gift but also to humbly submit to one another, in accordance with biblical teachings.

- **Time**

    Have you ever wondered why we can spend hours engrossed in a ball game, watching a movie, or enjoying leisure activities, but when it comes to attending church, we often expect to be in and out within thirty minutes to an hour? In many cases, our focus in church narrows down to a few songs and a sermon, with little room for the Holy Spirit to move as He sees fit. I've even been to churches where a timer on the back wall keeps a close watch to ensure the worship team or speaker doesn't exceed their allotted time. Unfortunately, these strict time schedules often prioritize shortening the service over allowing space for the gift of prophecy to operate within the congregation. This tendency reflects more concern about service duration than about God working in people's lives.

Consider this: What if today's church were instructed by Jesus to wait in the upper room for hours until the Holy Spirit descended upon them? How many would be glancing at their watches or trying to slip away? It's disheartening to witness the church hurrying God along. Perhaps if we surrendered our schedules and allowed time for God to move freely, we would experience a genuine outpouring of His presence and power.

- **Denominational barriers**

    One of the most prevalent causes of disdain for prophecy is the rejection of this gift and the office of a prophet by certain denominations. As I discussed earlier regarding erroneous doctrines, these denominations wield significant influence over what is taught and accepted.

- **Jezebel spirit**

    A Jezebel spirit within the church poses a threat to the spiritual gifts. Numerous churches fear the potential infiltration of this spirit and, as a result, choose to completely curtail the practice of prophecy. We will delve further into the topic of the Jezebel spirit in subsequent chapters of this book.

- **Antichrist spirit**

    The adversary is actively working to hinder people's freedom by suppressing the use of spiritual gifts. The spirit aligned with the Antichrist is already present on Earth, and it is striving to undermine the church by instigating its rejection of anything associated with the Holy Spirit or spiritual gifts. This Antichrist spirit aims to compel the church to renounce the power of God and adopt a more ritualistic and religious façade. Regrettably, this transformation is already occurring in numerous churches across the globe.

8

chapter

Freedom Without the Chaos

Local churches have strayed from their intended path, and within various denominations worldwide, we observe two contrasting extremes. On one side, there are churches that have forsaken the spiritual gifts in favor of adopting a religious spirit. In such congregations, there is minimal room for God to manifest His presence or for individuals to operate in their spiritual gifts. This starkly contradicts the practices of the early church and the teachings of Paul. Essentially, Christianity has been commodified to the extent that God's presence is often absent from the church experience. Instead, it has become more of a meticulously structured program aimed at entertaining attendees, rather than the sacred dwelling place of God and a house of prayer, as God originally intended it to be. A spirit of bondage seems to shackle the church, restraining the hands of God's people and muffling His voice. People typically attend these churches, engage in a few songs, listen to a brief sermon from the pastor, and leave without experiencing any significant spiritual transformation. This leads to a lack of ministry outside the church, as the saints are seldom able to exercise their spiritual gifts within the church environment. Unfortunately, this is the state of many churches globally, with a particularly prevalent manifestation in the United States, where a seeker-friendly approach often prevails over a Spirit-filled one.

> *1 Corinthians 14:6*
> *⁶ How is it then, brethren? when ye come together, every one of you hath a psalm, hath a doctrine, hath a tongue, hath a revelation, hath an interpretation. Let all things be done unto edifying.*

The other extreme we encounter is within charismatic churches, where there is an excessive fixation on spiritual gifts to the point of almost idolizing them. Instead of allowing God's sovereign movement, people in these churches tend to elevate the gifts themselves and those who administer them. Their primary pursuit becomes the spiritual exhilaration of being used by God in the gifts or receiving from the gifts, rather than earnestly worshiping Him and positioning themselves for His divine purposes. While it's essential to have freedom in the church, unchecked freedom can lead to chaos. There still exists a necessity for order within the church, including checks and balances to ensure the responsible use of spiritual gifts and to prevent harm to individuals. Regrettably, many individuals are delivering messages that do not align with God's will. Although they believe these messages to be from God, in numerous cases, they stem from their own thoughts or fleshly desires. In some instances, these messages might even be influenced by the enemy, leading to confusion or misguidance in people's lives.

I wholeheartedly endorse the principles outlined in 1 Corinthians 14, particularly the concept that prophets should submit to one another.

> *1 Corinthians 14:32-34*
> *32 And the spirits of the prophets are subject to the prophets.*
> *33 For God is not the author of confusion, but of peace, as in all churches of the saints.*
> *34 Let your women keep silence in the churches: for it is not permitted unto them to speak; but they are commanded to be under obedience as also saith the law.*

These verses are indeed thought-provoking. Take, for instance, verse 34, where Paul instructs women to remain silent in the church. This verse is often taken out of context, and it seems that Paul was addressing specific issues within that local church. Two key concerns arise: problems related to prophecy and women speaking excessively. These appear to be specific issues arising at a particular time in that congregation. From this, we can conclude that Paul was addressing the confusion within the church caused by both the misuse of prophecy and women talking excessively. It's possible that a spirit of rebellion was manifesting during that period. Therefore, it's important to note that this may not be a universal directive to all women in every church. Rather, it seems to be corrective guidance for those who were behaving disorderly, much like Paul's corrections regarding prophecy abuses.

The principle that "a prophet is subject to a prophet" emphasizes the importance of evaluating and judging prophetic messages. It's not uncommon to encounter prophets who operate independently, isolated from accountability or correction. In such cases, when there is no one to assess their teachings or prophetic utterances, errors can go unnoticed. Frequently, individuals may share prophecies in casual settings like parking lots, leaving no opportunity for leaders or other prophets to evaluate them. This loose use of prophecy can result in misunderstandings or misinterpretations of the message. Without witnesses, it becomes a matter of the prophet's word against the recipient's, potentially causing confusion and harm. To mitigate these issues, in our church services, we consistently create a space for prophecies to be shared openly and judged in the presence of the congregation. Transparency is vital, as God's messages should not be concealed. Additionally, when sharing corrective or directive prophecies, it's essential to exercise caution and, when necessary, involve a leader to prevent any confusion or misunderstanding.

I recall an incident when one of my children and their spouse attended our church but ceased attending afterward. It was only after several months, even years, that I learned the reason behind their absence. Someone had given them a prophetic word in the parking lot, which turned out to be inaccurate and created confusion, even accusing one of them of wrongdoing. This false prophecy caused them to leave our church. When abuses like these occur, they can tarnish the credibility of the gift, potentially making God appear untruthful. Although we know that God is not a liar, when people act in His name and deliver incorrect messages, it can harm the perception of His authenticity. Therefore, I insist on having witnesses present for prophecies to avoid such issues. It's those who must deal with the aftermath of these situations who understand the importance of these precautions. Just as pastors serve the congregation and are accountable for their teachings, so too should prophets be accountable to the church. The Bible underscores the principle of submitting to one another.

Ephesians 5:21
[21] *Submitting yourselves one to another in the fear of God.*

The final point I'd like to emphasize in this chapter is the importance of subjecting every prophecy to prayerful examination and testing. We must scrutinize prophecies through the guidance of the Holy Spirit, ensuring their alignment with the Word of God. Additionally, it's essential to discern the character of the person delivering the prophecy to ensure they are not deceiving us in any way. Sometimes, a period of prayer and spiritual warfare may be necessary to ascertain whether a particular word is genuinely from God and intended for our lives.

It's a common tendency among many Christians to hear words, teachings, or prophecies and immediately accept them without seeking confirmation through prayer and seeking God's guidance. Personally, I do not readily embrace every teaching I encounter unless I thoroughly study it and ascertain its authenticity. Likewise, I exercise caution when receiving prophetic words, only embracing them when I am certain they are from God. It is advisable to seek the input of other prophetic individuals who can assist in discerning whether a prophecy originates from God, the flesh, or the enemy. Furthermore, the received word should resonate with our own spirit, bearing witness to its truth and authenticity.

9 chapter

Build a Church that Allows the Holy Spirit to Move

There are several steps pastors can take to prepare the church environment for the orderly operation of spiritual gifts. Pastors should recognize that unless they actively foster the use of spiritual gifts, they may not manifest in the church. Failure to allow these gifts to function can hinder or even prevent the move of God, including signs, wonders, and miracles. So, what actions can pastors take to cultivate a healthy church atmosphere that encourages freedom and minimizes confusion?

It all begins with the leadership within the church. People tend to learn more from the actions and examples set by their leaders than from words alone. If the church leadership actively engages with and operates in spiritual gifts, the congregation is more likely to feel encouraged and empowered to do the same. However, some churches only allow leaders to operate in spiritual gifts while restricting the congregation.

To create an environment where the entire body can participate, leaders should promote the concept of a body ministry. When leadership supports and nurtures this idea, it encourages the congregation to operate in their spiritual gifts. Conversely, if the atmosphere is unsupportive or hinders the flow of the Holy Spirit, people may feel constrained in using their gifts.

Leaders should also actively encourage individuals to exercise their spiritual gifts during church services, not just in small group settings. While small groups can serve as valuable training grounds, the church service itself should provide opportunities for people to operate in their gifts. When the right structures and teachings are in place, there should be no fear in allowing God to use whomever He chooses within the congregation. After all, the church comprises the people, and each person is capable of hearing from God and ministering to others.

It is essential to create a safe environment for individuals to learn and grow in their spiritual gifts. As long as people are open to learning, receptive to correction, and willing to develop their gifts, pastors should encourage them to operate in their spiritual gifts within the church. This approach helps the church tap into the various aspects of God that are needed for its effective functioning. By enabling individuals to practice their gifts, pastors can equip them for ministry and ensure they are prepared for external service as well.

Ultimately, the key is to allow the Holy Spirit to move freely and according to His will. Allowing the Holy Spirit to use people and direct the church services results in order and edification. Disorder typically arises when personal agendas or fleshly motivations interfere. Pastors can help establish the necessary structure that allows the Holy Spirit to flourish within the church.

chapter 10
Put Structure and Protocols in Place

The significance of having structure in the context of spiritual growth cannot be emphasized enough. Much like children benefit from a structured environment in their homes, the church likewise thrives when it has a well-established framework. It's crucial to dispel the misconception that structure is detrimental. On the contrary, when church leaders set forth unambiguous expectations, provide guidelines for the proper exercise of spiritual gifts, and outline protocols for their use, it becomes possible to minimize potential issues. It's true that there may be individuals who choose to disregard these structures and protocols, leading to problems. Nevertheless, just as we address disciplinary matters with children in our homes, it is important to deal with similar situations within the church.

Here are some suggested methods to establish order:

1. Teach biblical truths and create the foundation
   - Teach on what prophecy is and what it looks like.
   - Teach on how to properly move in the gift of prophecy.
   - Teach what the bible says concerning prophecy and the prophets.
   - Teach what true prophecy looks like versus false prophecy.
   - Teach how to test prophecy and on the gifts of discernment.
   - Teach how to handle wrong prophecies.
   - Teach on the biblical requirements of a prophet (character, humility, dead to self)

2. Identify the prophets within your church:
   - Determine who should test the spirits or assess the given words.
   - Assess the reputation, character, and teachability of these prophets.
   - Evaluate whether they have personal agendas or improper motives.
   - Ensure these prophets are accountable and open to correction when they make mistakes.

3. Consider appointing a prophetic gatekeeper:
   - This role has proven effective in many churches.
   - Assign a person as the gatekeeper, responsible for receiving and assessing messages from individuals during worship.

- The prophetic gatekeeper should be experienced, sensitive to the Holy Spirit's leading, and able to maintain the flow.
- They can call upon individuals to share their words as guided by the Holy Spirit, ensuring that erroneous messages are not shared during the service.
- This approach maintains order in the church without suppressing the gifts.
- It may be beneficial to have a second person working with the gatekeeper to pray over the words together, but one person should be designated to call individuals forward according to God's order.
- Pastors should maintain a relationship with the prophetic gatekeepers and replace them if they become controlling or fearful.

4. Clearly define prophetic protocols for the church:
   - Prophecies can be shared during the service, but individuals should first consult with the prophetic gatekeeper.
   - Some words may require prayer at home and might not be relevant for the entire church, as they could be meant for an individual's personal guidance.
   - Praying over the word and seeking God's direction on how to share it should precede public proclamation.
   - The prophetic gatekeeper, guided by the Holy Spirit, will determine the appropriate timing for sharing the word.
   - Individuals should not be offended if they are not called to share a particular word. Sometimes multiple people receive the same message, but only one needs to deliver it, with others serving as confirmation.

5. Have a way to record the words for playback or write them down.
    - This protects the person giving the prophecy as well as the church.
    - Often times five people can hear the same prophecy, but hear different things.
    - Part of the prophetic is hearing by the Spirit and discerning what is true, what is for yesterday, what is for today and what is for tomorrow.
    - It provides proof of what is said

6. When receiving personal prophecies, maintaining order is crucial:
    - If multiple words are intended for the same individual, they should be shared together, avoiding confusion caused by alternating messages for different recipients.
    - Sensitivity and tact should be exercised while delivering prophetic words.
    - Individuals involved in known or ongoing sin should refrain from ministering to others.
    - It is essential to ensure one is not carrying transferable spiritual influences; deliverance should be sought before ministering to others.
    - Prophesying should be inspired by the Holy Spirit rather than imagination or other spirits.

7. Corrective words should be shared privately, in the presence of a leader, for obvious reasons.
    - Prophecies delivered outside of proper settings (e.g., parking lots) are not allowed.

- All prophecies must be witnessed and assessed before others.
- If a person is absent, the word should be written down or recorded and shared with the church leadership. It is risky to step outside the corporate anointing during a

chapter 11

Train, Equip, and Release

The value of effective training cannot be overemphasized. We often hear the saying, "knowledge is power," which can sometimes lead to a sense of pride. Much of what we believe we know may not be as solid as we think. Intellectual understanding does not necessarily equate to spiritual comprehension. The practical application of spiritual gifts, especially those of the Holy Spirit, involves real-life situations and a profound connection with God. Therefore, we should never underestimate the importance of teaching and guidance from the Holy Spirit.

In this regard, it's not enough to simply teach the biblical fundamentals of prophecy; we should also provide practical opportunities for individuals to exercise their prophetic gifts in a corporate setting. Initiating prophetic training, complete with chances to hear from God and minister to others, can make a significant difference. Prophetic leaders can play a pivotal role in nurturing these gifts instead of stifling them.

Structuring your training program should encompass not only the essential biblical principles of spiritual gifts and prophetic flow but also emphasize the cultivation of humility, accountability, and a willingness to accept correction. A well-rounded training program should address topics like handling offense, dealing with persecution and rejection, and nurturing a heart that remains in God's presence. Training should not be limited to prophets or prophetic individuals alone; it should become a norm within the church, where hearing from God through prophecy is expected.

Equipping individuals involves providing safe and supportive environments for them to share what they receive from the Holy Spirit. This can occur within church meetings, small group gatherings, or one-on-one mentoring relationships. Activation is a crucial component; faith without action is lifeless. By activating and using their spiritual gifts, individuals can strengthen and grow them. Therefore, refusing to allow the Holy Spirit to operate within the church setting hinders people from learning the practical "how" of prophecy before venturing outside the church's walls.

Once individuals understand the "why" and "how" of prophecy, they can be commissioned or sent out to serve. It's important to clarify that releasing someone to serve does not mean they have to leave the local church. In fact, every prophet or prophetic minister should have spiritual covering and accountability within their church community. Such leaders provide essential support and prayer as individuals engage in God's work.

Mentorship holds immense significance in today's church. Sending people out without proper support and accountability can expose them to spiritual pitfalls and dangers. Rather than allowing individuals to embark on their own, it's crucial to emphasize the importance of walking together with the support and guidance of established ministries.

Ministry is not a solo endeavor; we need a deep relationship with God and the protective covering of prayer and accountability to guard against error.

As the Bible teaches, when we train individuals in the way they should go, they will not depart from it. Imagine the impact of training people in the prophetic gift correctly, providing a solid foundation for others to follow. Instead of fearing the gift of prophecy, we can equip individuals to flow in it effectively and discerningly. Such training is invaluable, as prophecy serves as a powerful source of encouragement within the body of Christ, often providing the motivation to press on in one's faith journey.

In summary, the concepts of equipping, training, and releasing individuals into ministry are often misunderstood. Collaboration and accountability within a community are essential, as we are stronger together than when we go it alone. Even my wife and I are accountable to another ministry and leader, recognizing the necessity of such support. Therefore, I ask, who is your leadership covering?

Some of the areas we can focus on as part of the prophetic training are:

- How to hear God
- How do we know we are hearing God
- What to do with the visions and words we get
- Share examples of how God moves prophetically
- Do prophetic activation through laying on of hands
- Teach how to flow in the prophetic
- What to do with the prophecies you get for others
- Pitfalls and traps of prophecy
- Prophetic protocols

- Walking in prophetic order
- Humility and accountability
- Being teachable and correctible

Assign a prophetic mentor:

- Someone that they can share words, visions and dreams with
- An accountability and prayer partner
- An encourager that will help them grow prophetically
- Someone that can teach them in love

12
chapter

Encourage the Body to Operate in Prophecy

As I mentioned previously, providing encouragement is crucial for spiritual growth. Without proper encouragement and building up of individuals, many within the body of Christ may struggle to fulfill their God-given callings. Regrettably, churches often tend to focus on people's shortcomings instead of recognizing the gifts and callings present in their lives and actively assisting them in developing those areas. From my personal standpoint, it appears that our society tends to place more emphasis on what is wrong rather than what is right.

It's evident that numerous individuals within the body of Christ grapple with issues such as depression, a lack of peace, joy, and strength. I've frequently sought God's insight on this matter. Why is it that so many Christians find themselves in a state of despondency and fail to embrace the divine calling on their lives?

I believe that one of the contributing factors is the cessation of prophecy in many churches. The Bible tells us that speaking in tongues edifies the individual, whereas prophecy edifies the entire congregation. If this holds true, it stands to reason that the enemy seeks to obstruct the body of Christ from receiving encouragement and strength by attacking the prophetic ministry and gift. His objective is to gain control over people and impede the work of God. To counteract this strategy, we must demonstrate wisdom and discernment, opting to be sources of encouragement and exhortation. We should assist individuals in fulfilling everything that God has ordained for them. One of the greatest privileges I experience is identifying a gift or calling in someone and encouraging them to walk in it.

> *1 Corinthians 14:4*
> *[4] He that speaketh in an unknown tongue edifieth himself;*
> *but he that prophesieth edifieth the church.*

As leaders, we should serve as the most enthusiastic and supportive advocates that individuals have ever encountered. I firmly believe that we ought to embody the concept of servant leadership, dedicated to advancing and nurturing the kingdom of God. It saddens me to observe the current state of the church, where I frequently encounter two prevalent scenarios.

Firstly, there are church leaders who assume dictatorial roles, believing that they are the exclusive vessels through which God can minister. Consequently, they stifle the prophetic gifts in others and hinder the Holy Spirit's free movement. Their fears and controlling tendencies discourage the congregation from obeying the promptings of the Holy Spirit. The second scenario involves an unteachable and rebellious spirit within the church. Instead of submitting to spiritual authorities and adhering to godly order, some individuals exhibit a renegade attitude within the church, potentially causing disruptions. Both scenarios are detrimental, but encouragement plays a pivotal role in either direction, emanating from leadership to the congregation or from the congregation to the leadership.

Let's be honest; one of the most intimidating gifts to operate in is prophecy. There are individuals who harbor a strong aversion to prophecy and prophets. Thus, this presents a significant challenge. Additionally, engaging in prophecy demands substantial faith and patience in one's walk with God. Each time I venture into the prophetic realm, I am acutely aware of the risks involved. There is always the possibility that someone may dislike the message or reject the gift, perhaps even accusing me of delivering an erroneous word. I am immensely grateful for those who have provided encouragement and support in my ministry and giftings, even during moments when I have made mistakes.

The fear of making mistakes or delivering inaccurate prophecies often deters individuals from embracing the prophetic calling that God has placed upon their lives. Having leaders who guide and encourage us throughout this journey is invaluable. It provides a safety net, ensuring that when we do make mistakes, there are individuals who can help us learn from those experiences so that we can improve. I don't know any minister who has not made a mistake or missed God on occasion. This is precisely why we need one another for both accountability and encouragement.

13

chapter

Have the Church and Prophets Judge the Words

When we encounter the word "judge," it often carries negative connotations, as nobody likes to be subjected to judgment. The reason for this is that when you are judged, you are essentially at the mercy of the one passing judgment. If the judge is righteous, you can expect a fair and just evaluation. However, there are instances of unrighteous judges who pass judgment with a critical spirit. They show little mercy or compassion and often hold others to standards they themselves do not uphold. Their focus is not on truth but on control. Such wrong judgments and attitudes have no place in our churches.

Nevertheless, there is another kind of judgment, one that assesses talents or abilities, for example. This form of judgment provides constructive feedback aimed at helping individuals improve continually. The intention behind this type of judgment is not condemnation but education. I would refer to the person offering such guidance as a coach rather than a judge. This is why we need more "coaches" in the Kingdom of God. Coaches provide honest assessments and highlight areas for improvement, turning judgment into teachable moments.

When we judge a prophetic word, we are evaluating it not only for accuracy but also for the spirit in which it is delivered. Instead of shutting down the operation of spiritual gifts in our services, we should pray for discernment to rightly discern the word of God and address any counterfeits that may arise. It's about discernment rather than personal opinion or preference. Striking a balance between allowing God to move, sharing words, and maintaining order while addressing anything contrary to the working of the Holy Spirit is a genuine challenge for most churches.

I believe that nearly every church struggles with this balance. There's always a risk of error or the enemy gaining a foothold when we allow the operation of spiritual gifts. However, instead of shutting down the gifts or those whom God uses, we should learn to address and correct situations that are out of order, all in a spirit of love. These moments can serve as valuable examples to help individuals grow in their gifts and learn from correction.

In my personal experience, I have witnessed two extremes during my journey. Some churches completely shut down spiritual gifts, while others allow anything to go, which, in my opinion, can be equally if not more detrimental. We should pray for a sense of order in our churches, but not the kind of order that stifles the gifts. Rather, we should seek an order that aligns with the Word of God and teaches us how to operate in decency and order.

As God's people, I believe we need to work closely together in this area, striving for the Acts 2-type experiences where everyone contributes a word, a song, a testimony, or whatever the Holy Spirit desires for that particular meeting. The Holy Spirit can disrupt our services at times, as He does not endorse our religious practices or traditions. He desires complete control and the freedom to move as He pleases.

There is limited teaching on how to judge the move of the Spirit in churches. This is a matter that leaders should earnestly pray about, so that the Holy Spirit can bring revival and restoration to His people. Many churches have either succumbed to religious control and practices or have permitted things to spiral out of control, tolerating individuals operating in the flesh or soulish realm. The Acts chapter 2 church maintained visible order without stifling the Holy Spirit, allowing God to use or operate through anyone He pleased. Power coupled with order is always more effective than chaos without structure.

For the church to return to God's original intention, we must be willing to subject ourselves to proper judgment. The spirit of rebellion refuses accountability to anyone, which is a dangerous path to walk. Refusing to submit to authority or operate without accountability can lead to error or the acceptance of false doctrines. God established order to protect us, not to limit us, which is why we should welcome His judgment and correction within the church.

Additionally, it is crucial to remember that prophets should be accountable to the church. As stated in 1 Corinthians 14:32-33, "And the spirits of the prophets are subject to the prophets. For God is not the author of confusion, but of peace, as in all churches of the saints." This accountability ensures order and prevents confusion within the body of believers. Then in *1 Corinthians 14:29 it says Let the prophets speak two or three, and let the other judge.* The bible is clear that prophecy requires judging for accuracy and by what spirit it comes from.

Some of the ways we should judge words:

- Was the word accurate?
- Did it bear witness with the person spoken to?
- Was it a word that should have been released to the person at all?
- Was it given in the right spirit?
- Was the person giving it credible and right with God?
- Was there another spirit behind the word?
- Did the person only speak what God said, or did they add to or take away from the word released?
- Was it a word that should have been given at that time, or should it have been prayed about more?
- Was the word really for the person who was giving it versus who they gave it to?
- Was the word a corrective one that should have been done privately with the leadership present?

14

chapter

How to Correct and When to Correct

As leaders, we must not be driven by fear of others. One of the significant mistakes I've made in ministry occurred when I hesitated to confront individuals. I believed I was acting out of love, but in reality, it was fear of confrontation or fear of people that held me back. From my experiences, I've learned that addressing issues promptly is crucial, rather than allowing them to escalate. The fear of people's opinions, the desire to be liked, or the need to keep the peace can prevent us from correcting those who are out of line. There is a genuine risk that our failure to correct or delayed correction can lead to the misuse of gifts or positions, and others may begin to deviate from God's order. If we wait too long to correct, God might eventually teach us a lesson, as there are consequences to avoiding correction. People can get hurt, the church can become divided, or errors can seep in. Regardless, it's essential to remember that a loving father disciplines those he loves, so we should not withhold correction when it's needed.

However, it's important to clarify that there are times when God does not require us to correct but allows individuals to learn from their mistakes. Yet, when their actions affect others, correction becomes necessary, and it should be done in a spirit of love. Correcting others involves two key steps. First, we must be willing to correct when God prompts us to do so. Second, we should know how to correct people properly. Often, our approach to correction is influenced by how we were corrected in the past, but this may not be the best approach. Personal factors such as our past experiences, emotional wounds, and spiritual growth may affect our ability to correct effectively. It's crucial to empathize with the person being corrected, consider their perspective, intentions, and circumstances, and take into account factors like timing, location, privacy, personality, maturity, and the specific situation.

Correction should always be aimed at restoration or coaching rather than condemnation. We should remember that we, too, are works in progress and constantly in need of God's correction. When approaching someone for correction, seek God's heart for that person, speak His words, not your opinions, and be prepared for possible resistance or defensiveness. Reassure the individual that you care about their well-being and are trying to help them. If they display a rebellious or unteachable spirit, it may be necessary to stand your ground in love. Unwarranted emotional reactions should not deter us; truth delivered in love should remain our standard. Following correction, we should be willing to teach, encourage, and pray for the person.

Lastly, there are situations where it is wise to bring a witness when delivering correction. I've witnessed instances where individuals receiving correction later misrepresented what was said or done. In some cases, people have left the church and taken others with them, spreading lies about the correction process. Therefore, it's a wise practice for leaders to have a witness present during correction to prevent any misrepresentation that could be used to divide or harm the church.

15
chapter

Know who Labors Among You

The Bible instructs us to have a deep understanding of those who work alongside us in our faith journey. However, many churches tend to assign roles and positions to individuals without taking the time to truly know them on a personal and spiritual level. This practice carries a significant risk when we fail to invest the effort in getting to know people and discerning their spiritual disposition. Personally, I make it a priority to build relationships with potential speakers whom I invite to share in our church. I recall a testimony from a pastor that illustrates this point.

In this pastor's experience, his church pressured him to invite a renowned prophet as a guest speaker. This prophet had a reputation for delivering accurate prophecies, including names, phone numbers, and addresses. Instead of seeking divine guidance and praying about the matter, the pastor yielded to the congregation's demands and extended an invitation to the prophet. The pastor recounted that he picked up the guest prophet from the airport and dropped him off at the hotel to rest and prepare for the evening service. However, a few hours before the service, the pastor felt a strong prompting to visit the prophet at the hotel. The prophet was unaware of the pastor's early arrival.

Upon approaching the prophet's hotel room, the pastor noticed that the door was slightly ajar. To his surprise, he could see smoke emanating from the room. Out of concern, he naturally pushed the door open and entered. To his astonishment, he found the prophet standing in the midst of a circle of candles, earnestly invoking demons and inviting them to possess him for the upcoming meeting. The pastor was taken aback by this disturbing sight and immediately confronted the prophet, subsequently canceling the scheduled meeting.

This story serves as a powerful reminder that the ability to provide accurate information or access hidden knowledge does not necessarily imply a connection to the Holy Spirit. It highlights the importance of discernment and spiritual insight when evaluating individuals who claim to operate in the spiritual realm. Some individuals may be sourcing their information from malevolent spiritual forces, and it is vital for us to exercise discernment and wisdom in such matters.

We need to know who we are working with or receiving from.

> *1 Thessalonians 5:12*
> *[12] And we beseech you, brethren, to know them which labor among you and are over you in the Lord; and admonish you.*

I find it intriguing that we must not only be discerning about those we collaborate with but also those who hold authority over us and from whom we receive guidance. Surprisingly, I had previously overlooked this aspect of the verse. It is essential to recognize that being ordained as an apostle, prophet, pastor, teacher, or evangelist does not automatically guarantee that one is divinely sent by God or free from sin. In fact, some individuals ordain anyone and everyone without seeking the guidance of the Holy Spirit. In reality, ordination is not an act performed by humans; it is a divine appointment by God. God is the one who selects and designates individuals for specific roles.

However, the unfortunate reality is that many individuals employ these titles to attract followers, even if they lack divine calling or authorization. Consequently, we must exercise caution and discernment. Blindly following human leaders is not advisable. Instead, we should seek to hear from God and gain a deep understanding of the character and authenticity of those who hold leadership positions.

What we should know about who we labor with:

- Is the person living a Godly life?
- Is there known sin in their life?
- IS the person under authority and do they have a pastor?
- Is the person correctible and teachable?
- Is the person humble and do they demonstrate the love of Christ?
- Is the person Holy Spirit led or carnally minded?
- Does the person have a relationship with the leadership?
- Do their words line up with the word of God?
- Do their words come to pass?
- Does the person have the right motives and heart?
- Is the person seasoned in terms of how to present the word?
- Does the person have a spirit of pride?

- Is the person trying to create a following?
- Does the person value the other offices and gifts?

To be honest, God provides us with numerous warnings concerning individuals, but some of us tend to dismiss them because we prefer to believe the best about people. However, practicing discernment means that we allow God to safeguard us, recognizing that He possesses the knowledge of who is for us and who is against us, even when we may not be aware of it. It should be evident that certain individuals are influenced by spirits that are intended to undermine the church. Among these spirits are Jezebel, Absalom, Rebellion, Witchcraft, and even Take-Over spirits. It's challenging to confront what we cannot perceive, but God has the ability to reveal the spiritual forces at work. Often, He accomplishes this by granting us insight into the individuals we collaborate with. Spending time with people frequently leads to them inadvertently revealing their true nature. As the Bible states, "Out of the abundance of the heart, the mouth speaks."

16
chapter
The Jezebel Spirit

I touched upon this topic briefly in my previous chapter, but I would like to delve deeper into some of the spirits that attempt to infiltrate the church. Most of the time, these spirits collaborate with false prophecy or the disregard for prophecy in an effort to thwart the move of God.

The first spirit is Jezebel. If we delve into history, we will discover that Jezebel was not ignorant of prophecy or prophets. She maintained a group of 450 prophets of Baal and harbored a deep resentment toward God's prophets, even seeking their destruction. Her animosity was so intense that it drove the prophet Elijah to seek refuge under a Juniper tree, contemplating death. When the spirit of Jezebel infiltrates a church, it shifts the focus from Christ to the individual. Many individuals under the influence of this spirit may appear highly spiritual, amassing followers who seek their spiritual guidance and counsel. This spirit abhors true prophecy but is willing to employ false prophecy as a means of control and manipulation. It may cozy up to the pastor or launch attacks through others. Jezebel's objective is to undermine those in positions of authority, ultimately leading to division or destruction within the church. If left unchecked by the church's leaders, this spirit can quickly gain credibility and influence.

It is imperative to address this spirit promptly, as failing to do so can result in significant damage and fallout from its covert operations. Jezebel will feign friendliness while secretly undermining those in leadership. Furthermore, it is common to see this spirit accompanied by a spirit of mockery, which torments the church's leadership and derides them behind the scenes. The challenge with Jezebel is that her cunning nature often conceals her presence until it's too late, and the damage is already extensive.

> *Revelation 2:20*
> *[20] Notwithstanding I have a few things against thee, because thou sufferest that woman Jezebel, which calleth herself a prophetess to teach and to seduce my servants to commit fornication, and to eat things sacrificed unto idols.*

The term "fornication" carries a significant weight, but I believe that the Jezebel spirit's modus operandi is to allure individuals into conforming to worldly ways rather than maintaining their relationship with God and adhering to the order within the local church. Jezebel's ultimate aim is to steal the affections of the people she seduces, leading them away from the local church and distancing them from their relationship with Christ. The casualties resulting from Jezebel's manipulation and seduction are numerous and not to be taken lightly. Countless churches have experienced division and even destruction, with many pastors feeling betrayed by those under the influence of this spirit. Regrettably, most of these individuals are unaware of their deception and may even defend their actions instead of recognizing the truth. Jezebel is highly adept at deceiving others, leading them astray by propagating falsehoods. It is crucial for local intercessors to remain vigilant, as this spirit operates through various individuals and ministries. This spirit is undeniably one of the most perilous challenges the church faces, as it fosters a spirit of rebellion and false prophecy with the explicit intent of undermining the church's foundation.

Some of the signs someone is operating with a Jezebel spirit:

- They demonstrate manipulative behavior
- They are controlling and dominating
- They operate in a spirit of pride or false humility
- They may use seduction or operate in a spirit of immorality
- They are rebellious towards authority
- They operate in jealousy and envy
- They gossip and/or have backroom private discussions
- They swear you to secrecy
- They draw people unto themselves or into their group
- They tend to prophesy one on one or away from others
- They disrupt or interfere with relationships
- They cause division
- They may have false prophecies or teaching
- They lack repentance
- They may have a charismatic personality
- They may act lowly, but behind the scenes they are more bold
- They may act super spiritual
- They try to get close to the leadership, especially the pastor
- They seek a title, position or power

chapter 17

The Ahab Spirit

I understand that the Jezebel spirit often receives the most attention, which is quite appropriate. However, it's essential not to disregard the role of the Ahab spirit in empowering Jezebel. Jezebel couldn't thrive without an Ahab spirit enabling her. I've witnessed this dynamic frequently within the church, and honestly, this spirit tends to target pastors. Pastors, if not cautious, may find themselves walking on eggshells around certain individuals in the church, rather than enforcing order when it's necessary. In fact, many pastors struggle with a people-pleasing spirit that aligns itself with the Ahab spirit. The enemy exploits fear to persuade pastors that it's best to remain silent and avoid addressing certain behaviors in the church. Unfortunately, their failure to correct paves the way for Jezebel to function and even flourish.

I understand the reasoning behind pastors' hesitation – they're trying to grow the church and may fear that addressing issues will drive people away. However, in reality, they're setting the stage for Jezebel to seize control of the church. In my experience, leaders must remain vigilant and, when necessary, confront and correct to maintain order within the church. Jezebel seeks weak leaders she can influence and manipulate behind the scenes. The Jezebel spirit often spends more time with the congregation than the pastor does, becoming privy to all the church's issues and challenges. Then, after the pastor's failure or when issues arise, Jezebel uses that failure to destroy the leadership and scatter the sheep.

Just as Ahab was the king, not Jezebel, pastors are leaders, but they must not relinquish their authority to a demonic spirit or even to individuals influenced by such spirits. Ahab's downfall was his failure to stand up to Jezebel; she wore the pants in the family. If he had asserted his leadership, perhaps the fate of the prophets she sought to kill might have been different. The same holds true in the church — we cannot stand idly by while the Jezebel spirit seeks to destroy the sheep. It's our responsibility to cover and protect them. God will hold us accountable if we fail to defend those He has entrusted to us.

It's disheartening to see that many people in the church are not alert to deception. In fact, I believe that the gift of discernment is sorely lacking in the body of Christ. Too many wolves in sheep's clothing have infiltrated the church and deceived many. One clear symptom of this is the prevalence of gossip and side conversations that draw people away from the local church. Ahab had the power to intervene and stop Jezebel at any time, but he chose to turn a blind eye as she ruled his kingdom. Pastors must not allow the spirit of Ahab to take over their ministry. They must step up as the leaders God has called them to be. Ministry is not a popularity contest, and while some may leave, the foundation will remain unshaken.

Here are some signs that someone is operating in an Ahab spirit:

- They are reluctant to correct others
- They compare themselves to others
- They like to please others or have an extreme need to make others happy
- They are afraid of rejection
- They never take responsibility for things in their life and blame it on others
- They have private sin, but on the surface, they look good
- They do something wrong, but then try to do something to try to make up for the hurts they caused without dealing with the real issue.
- They believe that if someone is angry with them then it must be their own fault
- They have a habit of giving up their identity to bring peace at any price
- They feel like a failure or unaccepted
- They see faults in others and blame them for whatever is wrong
- They come across selfless, but are selfish
- They want to look good to others
- They give away power or authority in order for people to validate their identify
- They are difficult to talk to because they take everything as rejection
- They fish for compliments and want to be seen or noticed
- They are depressed because they never deal with the feelings they have buried
- They usually struggle to forgive themselves or receive God's forgiveness

vigilant and, when necessary, confront and correct to maintain order within the church. Jezebel seeks weak leaders she can influence and manipulate behind the scenes. The Jezebel spirit often spends more time with the congregation than the pastor does, becoming privy to all the church's issues and challenges. Then, after the pastor's failure or when issues arise, Jezebel uses that failure to destroy the leadership and scatter the sheep.

Just as Ahab was the king, not Jezebel, pastors are leaders, but they must not relinquish their authority to a demonic spirit or even to individuals influenced by such spirits. Ahab's downfall was his failure to stand up to Jezebel; she wore the pants in the family. If he had asserted his leadership, perhaps the fate of the prophets she sought to kill might have been different. The same holds true in the church – we cannot stand idly by while the Jezebel spirit seeks to destroy the sheep. It's our responsibility to cover and protect them. God will hold us accountable if we fail to defend those He has entrusted to us.

It's disheartening to see that many people in the church are not alert to deception. In fact, I believe that the gift of discernment is sorely lacking in the body of Christ. Too many wolves in sheep's clothing have infiltrated the church and deceived many. One clear symptom of this is the prevalence of gossip and side conversations that draw people away from the local church. Ahab had the power to intervene and stop Jezebel at any time, but he chose to turn a blind eye as she ruled his kingdom. Pastors must not allow the spirit of Ahab to take over their ministry. They must step up as the leaders God has called them to be. Ministry is not a popularity contest, and while some may leave, the foundation will remain unshaken.

Here are some signs that someone is operating in an Ahab spirit:

- They are reluctant to correct others
- They compare themselves to others
- They like to please others or have an extreme need to make others happy
- They are afraid of rejection
- They never take responsibility for things in their life and blame it on others
- They have private sin, but on the surface, they look good
- They do something wrong, but then try to do something to try to make up for the hurts they caused without dealing with the real issue.
- They believe that if someone is angry with them then it must be their own fault
- They have a habit of giving up their identity to bring peace at any price
- They feel like a failure or unaccepted
- They see faults in others and blame them for whatever is wrong
- They come across selfless, but are selfish
- They want to look good to others
- They give away power or authority in order for people to validate their identify
- They are difficult to talk to because they take everything as rejection
- They fish for compliments and want to be seen or noticed
- They are depressed because they never deal with the feelings they have buried
- They usually struggle to forgive themselves or receive God's forgiveness

- They are over merciful, overlooking too much
- They blame themselves when others betray or attack them
- They will do anything to gain acceptance
- They spend too much energy trying to impress others

18 chapter

The Absalom Spirit

As we delve deeper into the topic of maintaining order in the church and laying the foundation for the proper use of prophecy, we must also remain vigilant against another spirit – the Absalom spirit. This is a spirit I've personally encountered in ministry, and it closely relates to the rampant spirit of rebellion present in the church today.

Who was Absalom? He was the son of David, and the Bible tells us that he attempted to steal his father's throne. Absalom did not follow the established order; he didn't wait for his turn to become king. Instead, he sought to take what rightfully belonged to his father. Impatience characterized his actions, as he gathered supporters and followers to plan an uprising against David. Imagine your own son attempting to take everything that God helped you acquire through years of trials, tests, work, and obedience to Christ. Suddenly, someone within your own household seeks to seize it from you.

The key to understanding Absalom lies in his ability to turn David's own people against him. What's even more significant is that he had a seemingly valid reason as justification for attacking his father. His sister had been raped by her half-brother Amnon, and this heinous act filled him with anger. Instead of entrusting the matter to David, he took matters into his own hands and used it as fuel for his rebellion. While the rape was a terrible crime, and Amnon should have been punished, Absalom's approach was out of order. Unfortunately, David failed to address Amnon's sin, which was a mistake on his part.

A similar pattern unfolds in the church. When someone within the congregation commits wrongdoing, and if the pastor is unaware of it or fails to take action, an individual with the Absalom spirit becomes offended. They then gather people around them to share in their offense and attempt to overthrow the pastor. Rather than following the proper order, the Absalom spirit seizes the opportunity to attack the church. Those aligned with the Absalom spirit often side with it, failing to objectively assess the situation or seek resolution through prayer. Accusations and judgments frequently accompany this spirit. Absalom's anger over perceived injustice spreads to his followers, who become equally incensed and offended by the same issues that fuel him against his father.

How can we combat this spirit? One approach is to maintain order and provide correction. Individuals with the Absalom spirit are often unteachable and naturally inclined to rebel. It's crucial to test individuals in your ministry to determine if they are correctable and teachable. I've made the mistake of not doing so in the past, only to realize the true nature of the person after correction or addressing issues. The Absalom spirit is frequently intertwined with pride. Therefore, a humble and teachable person should not be offended by correction. Don't shy away from teaching and correction to appease people; just remember to administer them with love, and you will soon identify where these spirits are at work.

Here are some indicators someone has an Absalom spirit:

- They may have big dreams, but they blame other people for blocking those dreams
- They feel that they are not heard, or their level of wisdom is being ignored by leadership
- They feel their gifts are not being properly used by leadership
- They get angry if they are not recognized for their contributions
- They have big dreams, but blame others, for blocking those dreams
- They have hidden disappointments, unresolved offenses, bitterness, and anger
- They have hidden agendas, strategies, and secret alliances
- They have their own standards and criteria for judging situations that do not line up with the word of God
- They have a fault finding or critical spirit
- They have a form of false humility
- They think they are wiser than the leadership

own people against him. What's even more significant is that he had a seemingly valid reason as justification for attacking his father. His sister had been raped by her half-brother Amnon, and this heinous act filled him with anger. Instead of entrusting the matter to David, he took matters into his own hands and used it as fuel for his rebellion. While the rape was a terrible crime, and Amnon should have been punished, Absalom's approach was out of order. Unfortunately, David failed to address Amnon's sin, which was a mistake on his part.

A similar pattern unfolds in the church. When someone within the congregation commits wrongdoing, and if the pastor is unaware of it or fails to take action, an individual with the Absalom spirit becomes offended. They then gather people around them to share in their offense and attempt to overthrow the pastor. Rather than following the proper order, the Absalom spirit seizes the opportunity to attack the church. Those aligned with the Absalom spirit often side with it, failing to objectively assess the situation or seek resolution through prayer. Accusations and judgments frequently accompany this spirit. Absalom's anger over perceived injustice spreads to his followers, who become equally incensed and offended by the same issues that fuel him against his father.

How can we combat this spirit? One approach is to maintain order and provide correction. Individuals with the Absalom spirit are often unteachable and naturally inclined to rebel. It's crucial to test individuals in your ministry to determine if they are correctable and teachable. I've made the mistake of not doing so in the past, only to realize the true nature of the person after correction or addressing issues. The Absalom spirit is frequently intertwined with pride. Therefore, a humble and teachable person should not be offended by correction. Don't shy away from teaching and correction to appease people; just remember to administer them with love, and you will soon identify where these spirits are at work.

Here are some indicators someone has an Absalom spirit:

- They may have big dreams, but they blame other people for blocking those dreams
- They feel that they are not heard, or their level of wisdom is being ignored by leadership
- They feel their gifts are not being properly used by leadership
- They get angry if they are not recognized for their contributions
- They have big dreams, but blame others, for blocking those dreams
- They have hidden disappointments, unresolved offenses, bitterness, and anger
- They have hidden agendas, strategies, and secret alliances
- They have their own standards and criteria for judging situations that do not line up with the word of God
- They have a fault finding or critical spirit
- They have a form of false humility
- They think they are wiser than the leadership

chapter 19

The Spirit of Witchcraft

Many churches are under attack by witchcraft, but often remain unaware of this insidious threat. Witchcraft is currently the fastest-growing religion in the world, with witches found in various places, including within local congregations. Unfortunately, many Christians are oblivious to this reality. In some instances, we inadvertently allow individuals practicing witchcraft to lay hands on us, offer guidance in our lives, or even speak curses upon us. This highlights the need for church leaders to possess greater wisdom and discernment.

It's crucial to recognize that one doesn't need official certification as a witch to engage in witchcraft. Ungodly prayers, manipulative prayers, and the presence of controlling and rebellious spirits are all aspects of witchcraft. Some might even argue that gossip and slander can be considered forms of witchcraft.

Demonic tongues can also be utilized in prayers, releasing witchcraft. The spirit of witchcraft carries with it confusion and a heavy spiritual atmosphere that affects both church leadership and the congregation. Although Jezebel practiced open witchcraft, it often went unrecognized as such. In numerous prayer meetings, I've heard individuals pray curses upon others instead of speaking God's will over them. For instance, they might pray, "Lord, I ask that you cause them to lose their job or experience health issues until they repent." Such prayers are nothing short of witchcraft emerging from the lips of a believer.

Instances of people speaking ill of church leadership and engaging in gossip also fall under the category of witchcraft. At times, genuine witches infiltrate the church, masquerading as believers. Their tongues, prayers, and even their dance and worship exude a demonic influence. They come with the intention to cause pain and harm, aiming to disrupt the move of God and negatively impact the operation of spiritual gifts. The church must confront and quell the spirit of witchcraft, as it poses a significant threat capable of destroying both leadership teams and congregations alike.

Signs that there is active witchcraft is coming against you:

- **You feel like you are being watched**

    Witches will monitor people in the spirit, even astral projecting if necessary to spy on people or attack them in their sleep. Monitoring spirits are like the devil's private investigators. You can't see them, but they can see and hear you. The devil is not omnipresent or omniscient, so he depends on monitoring spirits to gather information.

- **You start getting clumsy, drop things or have frequent accidents**

    People that are not normally clumsy will start dropping things or tripping over things when they never did before.

- **You will start to lose your motivation, drive and excitement**

    The spirit of witchcraft will demoralize you and demotivate you. You will lose your drive and ambition for life or the things of God. You will start feeling like there is no hope and you may put off things you would have got done in the past. You may not even want to minister any more.

- **You can't seem to hear from God**

    You used to be able to hear from God, but now it's like God isn't talking to you anymore. No matter how much you pray it feels like He is not listening.

- **You start hearing or seeing things you didn't before**

    All the sudden you are hearing voices or seeing figures you didn't before. These voices can bring confusion, fear and anxiety.

- **You feel depressed or oppressed.**

    It will feel like a dark cloud is over you and you can't get away from it. A heaviness will be on you for no reason. Depression even speaking to you. Some people may even be visited by a spirit of suicide

- **You will have strange thoughts**

    All the sudden you don't trust others. You wonder who is for you and who is against you. You become more guarded because of the thoughts that you keep having.

- **The spirit of death will come to you**

    You will suddenly want to die, or feel like you are going to die. You may even feel sorry for yourself. Remember when Jezebel came against Elijah. He went and hid because that spirit chased after him. He even sat under a bush and asked God to take him.

- **You are forgetful**

    You can't seem to remember things and get easily confused by things you usually remember. It's like you are in a brain fog.

- **People take turns attacking you**

    Spirits of accusation start coming up from multiple people. You start getting attacked by numerous people. You can even see a pattern of attacks against you.

- **You feel like you are physically and mentally worn out**

    You are tired and feel like you have fatigue. Your mind is even tired of thinking about things.

- **You lose your identity**

    You forget who you are in Christ Jesus. Your flesh becomes stronger, and you feel disqualified from being used by God.

- **Nightmares and bad dreams**

    You start having bad dreams that you don't understand. Things you don't even want to speak out loud. Visions and pictures that get stuck in your mind.

- **Unable to sleep at night**

    You start to wrestle in your sleep. You start having difficulty going to sleep or staying asleep. You feel like you are fighting to sleep.

20
chapter

The Leviathan Spirit

The Leviathan spirit is a concept that may not be widely known among Christians. The term "Leviathan" is found in the Bible, particularly in the Old Testament, where it is often used metaphorically to represent a formidable and destructive force. This spirit primarily targets prophetic or apostolic ministries and draws its inspiration from a sea creature mentioned in the Book of Job, specifically in Job 41. In this chapter, a vivid and symbolic description of Leviathan is provided, emphasizing its strength, resilience, and fearsome nature.

Verses 1-9 in Job 41 describe Leviathan's appearance and power, highlighting its impervious characteristics. Verses 10-34 depict Leviathan's prowess in battle and the impossibility of subduing it through human means. This portrayal of Leviathan in Job 41 serves as a representation of potent and uncontrollable forces that can exist in both the natural and spiritual realms.

Furthermore, in Isaiah 27:1, Leviathan is described as a dragon. Psalm 74:4 seems to suggest that it not only takes the form of a dragon but also possesses multiple heads. Revelation 13:1-2 offers an even more detailed description of Leviathan, stating that it has seven heads, ten horns, ten crowns, and the name of blasphemy inscribed on its heads.

> *Job 41:1-34*
> *¹ Canst thou draw out leviathan with an hook? Or his tongue with a cord which thou lettest down?*
> *² Canst thou put an hook into his nose? or bore his jaw through with a thorn?*
> *³ Will he make many supplications unto thee? will he speak soft words unto thee?*
> *⁴ Will he make a covenant with thee? wilt thou take him for a servant for ever?*
> *⁵ Wilt thou play with him as with a bird? or wilt thou bind him for thy maidens?*
> *⁶ Shall the companions make a banquet of him? shall they part him among the merchants?*
> *⁷ Canst thou fill his skin with barbed irons? or his head with fish spears?*
> *⁸ Lay thine hand upon him, remember the battle, do no more.*
> *⁹ Behold, the hope of him is in vain: shall not one be cast down even at the sight of him?*
> *¹⁰ None is so fierce that dare stir him up: who then is able to stand before me?*
> *¹¹ Who hath prevented me, that I should repay him? whatsoever is under the whole heaven is mine.*
> *¹² I will not conceal his parts, nor his power, nor his comely proportion.*

[13] *Who can discover the face of his garment? or who can come to him with his double bridle?*

[14] *Who can open the doors of his face? his teeth are terrible round about.*

[15] *His scales are his pride, shut up together as with a close seal.*

[16] *One is so near to another, that no air can come between them.*

[17] *They are joined one to another, they stick together, that they cannot be sundered.*

[18] *By his neesings a light doth shine, and his eyes are like the eyelids of the morning.*

[19] *Out of his mouth go burning lamps, and sparks of fire leap out.*

[20] *Out of his nostrils goeth smoke, as out of a seething pot or caldron.*

[21] *His breath kindleth coals, and a flame goeth out of his mouth.*

[22] *In his neck remaineth strength, and sorrow is turned into joy before him.*

[23] *The flakes of his flesh are joined together: they are firm in themselves; they cannot be moved.*

[24] *His heart is as firm as a stone; yea, as hard as a piece of the nether millstone.*

[25] *When he raiseth up himself, the mighty are afraid: by reason of breakings they purify themselves.*

[26] *The sword of him that layeth at him cannot hold: the spear, the dart, nor the habergeon.*

[27] *He esteemeth iron as straw, and brass as rotten wood.*

²⁸ *The arrow cannot make him flee: slingstones are turned with him into stubble.*
²⁹ *Darts are counted as stubble: he laugheth at the shaking of a spear.*
³⁰ *Sharp stones are under him: he spreadeth sharp pointed things upon the mire.*
³¹ *He maketh the deep to boil like a pot: he maketh the sea like a pot of ointment.*
³² *He maketh a path to shine after him; one would think the deep to be hoary.*
³³ *Upon earth there is not his like, who is made without fear.*
³⁴ *He beholdeth all high things: he is a king over all the children of pride.*

Isaiah 27:1
¹ *In that day the Lord with his sore and great and strong sword shall punish leviathan the piercing serpent, even leviathan that crooked serpent; and he shall slay the dragon that is in the sea.*

Psalm 74:14
¹⁴ *Thou brakest the heads of leviathan in pieces, and gavest him to be meat to the people inhabiting the wilderness.*

Revelation 13:1-2
¹ *And I stood upon the sand of the sea, and saw a beast rise up out of the sea, having seven heads and ten horns, and upon his horns ten crowns, and upon his heads the name of blasphemy.*

²And the beast which I saw was like unto a leopard, and his feet were as the feet of a bear, and his mouth as the mouth of a lion: and the dragon gave him his power, and his seat, and great authority.

21
chapter
Be Watchful, Not Fearful

You might be wondering why a book on prophecy is delving into the spirits discussed in the recent chapters. The reason is quite straightforward. These are the primary spirits that target and undermine the prophetic gift and ministry within the church. The enemy's objective is to stifle prophecy and the operation of spiritual gifts. These divisive spirits aim to disrupt and harm the church and its leaders. We must remain vigilant and prayerful so that when we encounter these spirits, we are prepared to resist them. We cannot afford to give them any opportunity to hinder a move of God, as they are capable of preventing it. Many churches have been divided due to the influence of these spirits, sometimes leading to disagreements and strife among the congregation.

The church needs to be watchful and ready to engage in spiritual warfare when necessary. The enemy harbors a deep dislike for prophecy and holds an even greater animosity towards prophets. He will go to great lengths to discredit prophets and silence their voices, often using false prophets to divert people from the truth.

While vigilance is essential, we must not allow a spirit of fear to overcome us. We should not discard prophecy due to fear, nor should we allow the fear of error to lead us to quench the Holy Spirit and reject the gift of prophecy. This is precisely what the enemy desires for the church. He wants to render the church powerless and deaf to the guidance of the Holy Spirit. In essence, he is exploiting our fears to control the Holy Spirit's work in our lives and services. We must outsmart the enemy by maintaining the proper order in our churches, allowing the gifts of the Spirit to flow without fear of misuse or abuse. Church leaders bear the responsibility of equipping the body to fulfill God's work, and they should not let fear obstruct the move of God. Through the right order, the gifts of the Spirit can operate, leading to transformed lives.

22

chapter

Why Prophets and Pastors Often Clash

One of the significant concerns I have about the church pertains to the lack of collaboration among the five offices that God has ordained for the church. Instead of working together harmoniously, there seems to be a great deal of competition among ministers, churches, and giftings. This competition, I believe, is one of the reasons why we are not witnessing the move of God that we so desperately need today. We should be presenting a united front against the enemy and striving to reach as many people as possible for Christ.

However, what we often see is infighting, bickering, and even a sense of rivalry among ministers, some of whom build followings around themselves to elevate their own status rather than glorifying God. If we are genuinely dead to self, shouldn't we be partnering together to overcome the schemes of the devil? The devil is practically reveling in the disarray within the local church as it self-destructs and overlooks the move of God. I have observed situations where pastors drive prophets out of their churches, and/or prophets rising up against pastors, leading to division in the church. Both scenarios deeply grieve God.

Considering my dual role as both a pastor and a prophet, I have more insight in this area than many. Many individuals lay claim to the title of prophet, yet they fail to recognize the significance of the local church. In fact, some of them carry unresolved wounds and bitterness from past church experiences. Due to this, they crave autonomy and utterly reject the notion of being accountable to anyone. They not only spurn the idea of accountability but also rush to pass judgment on the local church and its pastors. In some cases, their reluctance to support or align with the local church stems from personal agendas and a thirst for the limelight. Some openly criticize the local church and may even advocate for people to abandon it in favor of home or travel ministries. Additionally, a significant number of these individuals pursue titles, attention, financial gain, or even fame, desiring adoration and, in some instances, idolization from others. Regrettably, they tend to resist walking in humility, remain unteachable, and reject correction. When confronted with their actions, they tend to react by fleeing or rebelling against those in positions of authority. In some cases, they go so far as to incite rebellion within the congregation, persuading many to follow their lead.

Similarly, there are numerous pastors who resist being held accountable to others. They desire to wield ultimate authority without any checks and balances. Some pastors develop a sense of ownership over the church, believing that the people belong to them, when, in reality, the church and its members belong to God. This is a clear error, but I often witness pastors expelling prophets from their churches in an attempt to maintain control. Some pastors justify this by claiming they are protecting the church, which I can understand when it's genuinely about safeguarding the congregation. However, many pastors employ this tactic to control the church or safeguard their positions instead of fostering unity with other leaders. In some instances, they even turn the congregation against the prophets by portraying them as threats or as being in error when that is not the case.

23 chapter

It's Time to Bring Order Back to the Church

The time has come to restore order within the church. In its infancy, the church was firmly established upon Jesus as our cornerstone, and it was built with a foundation that included apostles, prophets, pastors, teachers, and evangelists. Jesus must have had a profound reason for instituting these five offices, whether it was to anticipate divisions and errors within the church or to emphasize the importance of checks and balances. In any case, God has provided a structured order for the church to adhere to. He has presented guidelines in the Bible regarding the format of services, the acceptance of spiritual gifts, and the overall flow of church proceedings. Regrettably, the contemporary church bears little resemblance to its early counterpart. We have drifted away from fervent prayer, the movement of the Holy Spirit, and allowing God to work through His people. Instead, we have replaced the living and vibrant nature of the church with a meticulously controlled program. While it also addresses some issues that were happening during that time, 1 Corinthians 14 gives us a glimpse into what a church service should look like. Does your church allow the body of Christ to function? By bringing order back to the church, the atmosphere of the church will be set to allow God to move according to His will and purpose for this hour.

> *1 Corinthians 14:26-40*
> *²⁶ How is it then, brethren? when ye come together, every one of you hath a psalm, hath a doctrine, hath a tongue, hath a revelation, hath an interpretation. Let all things be done unto edifying.*
> *²⁷ If any man speak in an unknown tongue, let it be by two, or at the most by three, and that by course; and let one interpret.*
> *²⁸ But if there be no interpreter, let him keep silence in the church; and let him speak to himself, and to God.*
> *²⁹ Let the prophets speak two or three, and let the other judge.*
> *³⁰ If any thing be revealed to another that sitteth by, let the first hold his peace.*
> *³¹ For ye may all prophesy one by one, that all may learn, and all may be comforted.*
> *³² And the spirits of the prophets are subject to the prophets.*
> *³³ For God is not the author of confusion, but of peace, as in all churches of the saints.*
> *³⁴ Let your women keep silence in the churches: for it is not permitted unto them to speak; but they are commanded to be under obedience as also saith the law.*

[35]{.sup} And if they will learn any thing, let them ask their husbands at home: for it is a shame for women to speak in the church.

[36]{.sup} What? came the word of God out from you? or came it unto you only?

[37]{.sup} If any man think himself to be a prophet, or spiritual, let him acknowledge that the things that I write unto you are the commandments of the Lord.

[38]{.sup} But if any man be ignorant, let him be ignorant.

[39]{.sup} Wherefore, brethren, covet to prophesy, and forbid not to speak with tongues.

[40]{.sup} Let all things be done decently and in order.

Made in the USA
Middletown, DE
15 October 2024